Beneath the Waves

Contents

Deep-Sea Discovery	4
High-Rise Habitats	6
Giant Jellies	8
Gentle Giants	10
A Whale of a Time	14
Heavyweight Champs	15
Talk About Teeth	20
Dolphin Dives	22
Project Jonah	24
Save the Sea Cows	26
Splash Out	28
Glossary	30
Index	31
Discussion Starters	32

Features

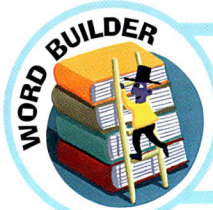

You probably know what a submarine is, but do you know what the two parts of this word mean? Find out on page 5.

Do you know that ships can accidentally take animals on board? Learn how this can affect a port area on page 9.

Without this underwater animal many great works of art and many famous books would not exist! Discover more on page 10.

It's time for a trip to the aquarium. Turn to **Splash Out** on page 28 and see what wonders are waiting for you!

What signs do whale-watchers look for?

Visit **www.infosteps.co.uk**
for more about **OCEAN MAMMALS**.

Deep-Sea Discovery

The oceans are the largest **habitats** on Earth. From the seashore to the sea floor countless creatures of all shapes and sizes scuttle, swim, dart and drift through the water.

Today people can explore and study ocean life and ocean landscapes like never before. Research ships, submarines, diving suits and oxygen tanks allow explorers to dive deeper than ever before. They can discover underwater worlds which once lay hidden and mysterious beneath the waves.

A fish and a diver meet face-to-face. What do you think the fish might be thinking?

WORD BUILDER

The word *marine* means "to do with the sea". The prefix *sub* means "under". A submarine is a vessel especially designed for moving about under the sea.

5

High-Rise Habitats

Giant kelp forests are home to hundreds of sea creatures. Some kelp forests tower many storeys high, like living skyscrapers in the sea. These forests are an important link in ocean **food chains**. They provide food and shelter for creatures as tiny as snails and as huge as whales.

Like many other forests on Earth, kelp forests change with the seasons. In winter wild waves rip the kelp from the rocks making the forest thinner. In spring new branches grow thick and fast making a fresh kelp canopy in just days.

Giant kelp forests grow in cold sunlit waters along the coasts of the United States, South Africa, Australia and New Zealand. Sea otters make their beds in kelp canopies off the United States.

A Kelp Forest Food Chain

1. Kelp leaves soak up sunlight for **photosynthesis** and the forest grows.

2. Visiting whales feed on **plankton** living in the kelp forest.

3. Sea animals such as snails nibble the kelp.

4. Fish, otters and other larger sea animals eat the small animals.

5. Sharks and seals hunt the larger sea animals.

6. Crabs and seastars feed on dead animals.

Giant Jellies

In many parts of an ocean, the water is lit by glow-in-the-dark jellyfish that pulse with a light of their own. Jellyfish can be brilliant colours. Some are striped, some are spotted and some are almost see-through.

Jellyfish belong to a family of animals called **invertebrates**. These amazing creatures may not have bones, brains, hearts or even eyes, but they pack a lot of power! The stinging cells on the tentacles of many jellies make them deadly predators.

Many jellyfish have special cells that produce light.

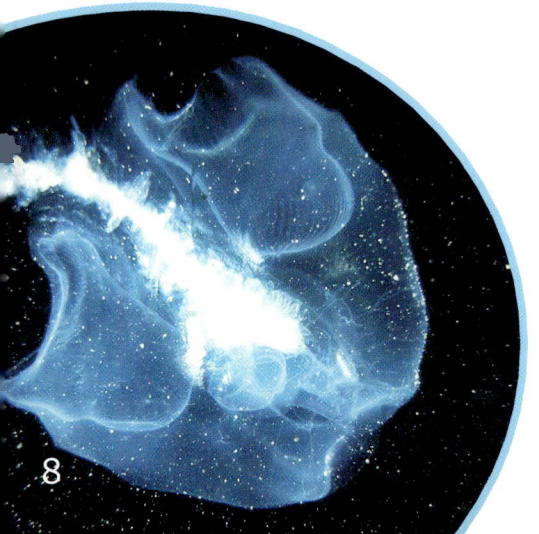

EARTH WATCH

Ships take in ballast water to keep them steady. Sometimes sea creatures such as jellyfish get sucked on board too. When the ship arrives at a new port, the water—and the jellyfish—are let out. Jellyfish can multiply quickly and eat all of the ocean food supply in an area. This can mean trouble for the local port area.

Tentacles

The giants of the jelly world have bodies larger than a beach umbrella and tentacles up to 30 metres long!

Gentle Giants

The giant octopus is a sea creature that scares some people. It can grow to be as long, from arm tip to arm tip, as a school bus. Long ago sailors told tales of these terrifying sea monsters leaping out of the water to sink sailing ships!

Today divers sometimes swim with these giants of the octopus world. They have learned that the giant octopus is not fierce. It is actually a shy, gentle and highly intelligent animal that feeds mostly on shellfish.

Eye

Tentacles

TIME LINK

The cuttlefish is a cousin of the octopus. When in danger it shoots out a cloud of brown ink. Without the cuttlefish many great works of art and many famous books would not exist. The brown ink called sepia was used long ago for drawing and writing.

An octopus can be tricky to find. Octopuses live alone, often hidden in a rocky cave or den. They leave leftover shells and bones at their den entrance.

A Whale of a Time

There is nothing like the sight of a 28-ton whale throwing itself out of the water to make you realize that the ocean is packed full of surprises. There are more than eighty different **species** of whales and they come in a wide range of sizes. Whales may have fins, flippers and tails, but they are mammals not fish. Like all mammals, whales are warm-blooded and feed their young milk. They must come up for air which they breathe through nostrils called blowholes.

Heavyweight Champs

When it comes to giants of the sea nothing beats the whale family. Blue whales are Earth's heavyweight champions. They are the largest animals on our planet.

There are two types of whales—toothed whales and baleen whales. All the largest whales are baleen whales. They use their baleen plates as strainers to catch millions of tiny ocean plants and animals called plankton and krill.

Baleen whale

Baleen plates stretch from a whale's upper to lower jaw.

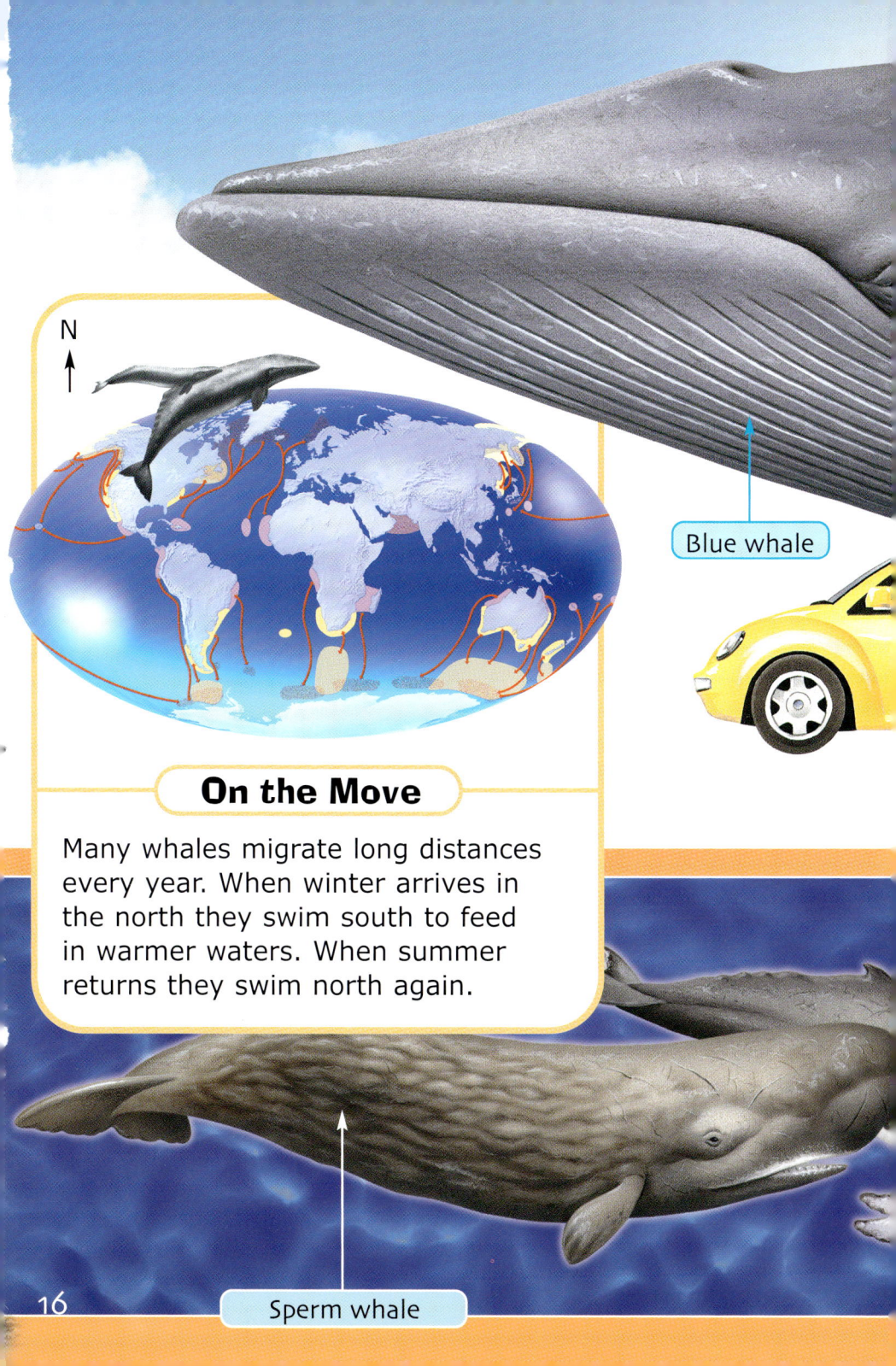

Blue whale

On the Move

Many whales migrate long distances every year. When winter arrives in the north they swim south to feed in warmer waters. When summer returns they swim north again.

Sperm whale

Gentle Giants continued

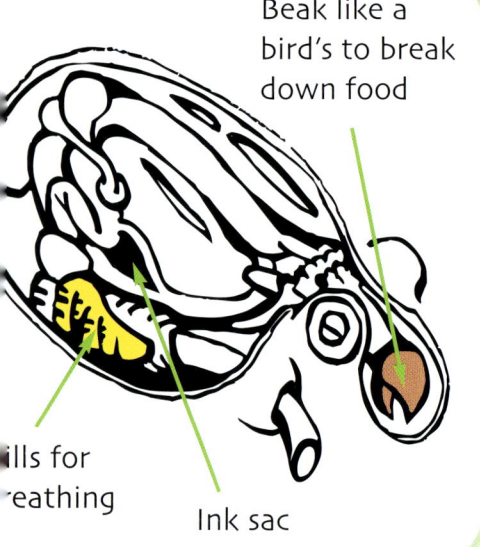

Beak like a bird's to break down food

Gills for breathing

Ink sac

An octopus is a fast and surprising swimmer. It swims backwards by suddenly squirting out a jet of water.

Suckers—An octopus has more than a thousand on each arm. They are used for tasting, touching and even smelling.

An octopus is an expert trickster. It can squirt ink or change the colour and texture of its skin to hide.

Humpback whales breach, or throw their huge bodies up out of the water, more than any other great whale. Some breach as many as 100 times in a row!

The Tale of a Whale

All whales have a layer of fat called blubber which stores energy and heat. People began hunting whales for their blubber nearly 1,000 years ago. During the late 1800s many kinds of whales were almost hunted to **extinction**.

Herman Melville (1819–1891)

Moby Dick is a story about a hunt for a great white whale. It is one of the most famous novels ever written. The author Herman Melville worked on whaling ships. In his novel he describes a hunt for a fierce white whale which sailors named Moby Dick.

Talk About Teeth

Most toothed whales are smaller than baleen whales. They include sperm whales, orcas, beluga whales, dolphins and porpoises. Most toothed whales eat fish or squid. They can dive to catch prey from the deepest darkest parts of the ocean.

Toothed whales have a special sense called **echolocation** that helps them find and track their prey. They scan the water with a series of slow clicks that become faster as the whales swim closer to their target.

 Canada

Beluga whales live in the icy Arctic Ocean and around Canada. Some people call these shy white whales "sea canaries". They have a special oil-filled hump on their head that makes their whistles and clicks sound like songs.

The sperm whale dives deeper than all other whales. It hunts giant squid. Giant squid are the world's largest invertebrates so they are quite a mouthful!

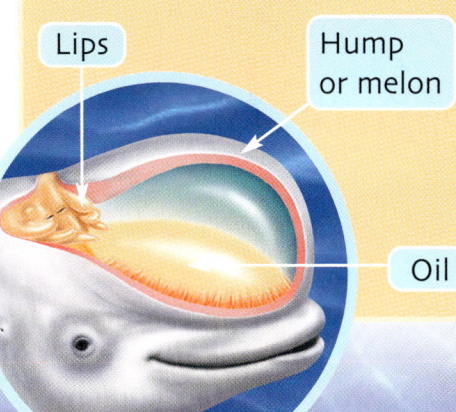

Lips — Hump or melon — Oil

What signs do whale-watchers look for?

Visit www.infosteps.co.uk for more about OCEAN MAMMALS.

21

Dolphin Dives

Dolphins are part of the whale family too. They are among the most playful and friendly creatures of the sea. Dolphins are often seen leaping and diving beside ships. They sometimes even surf the waves a ship makes as it slices through the water.

Dolphins swim in large family groups called pods. They look after one another and talk in a series of high-pitched whistles and clicks.

Dolphins have smooth sleek bodies designed for speed. They often leap out of the water in graceful arcs and land with a big splash.

EARTH WATCH

In 1993 a law was passed to ban drift-net fishing. People often used drift nets to catch tuna fish. These nets trapped and killed dolphins and other animals as well. Many companies now help protect dolphins by showing a "Dolphin Friendly" label on cans of tuna.

Project Jonah

In many parts of the world today laws protect whales and prevent people from hunting them. Whales sometimes get into trouble all on their own however. These underwater experts can become stranded high and dry on land.

This is when they need people to come to the rescue. Special groups such as Project Jonah have teams of trained workers who help save whales in trouble.

How to Help a Whale in Trouble

1. Stay calm. Call your local whale-rescue hotline. A marine medical team will soon be there.

2. Keep the whale cool by pouring water over it. Protect it from the sun with wet sheets. Never pour water down its blowhole.

3. Dig holes in the sand for the whale's flippers. Dig channels so the tide can reach it quickly.

4. Pat the whale gently. Do not rub it.

5. Talk softly or sing to the whale. Let it know you are a friend.

Save the Sea Cows

People are coming to the rescue of other sea mammals too. Manatees and dugongs are friendly gentle mammals that live in warm waters around the world. They eat plants in underwater meadows and are sometimes called sea cows. Manatees and dugongs are the only sea mammals that are **herbivores**.

Manatees (shown right) form close family ties. A manatee calf stays with its mother for many years. They play together and talk in squeaks and squeals.

Dugongs (shown right) live in the warm shallow waters of the Indian and southern Pacific oceans.

EARTH WATCH

Save the Sea Cows

Not so long ago manatees and dugongs were hunted for their meat, oil and skins. People are now working hard to save these gentle giants from extinction.

Splash Out at Blu

Come and explore the wonders of our ocean planet! Discover a whole new world at Bluewater Bay Aquarium. From the tiny creatures of shallow rock pools to the giants of the open seas, you'll be surprised by the animals you meet in our award-winning exhibits and hands-on habitats.

Look for the new arrivals at the penguin pool.

Fish of all shapes and sizes have room to roam in our jumbo-sized indoor ocean tank.

Aquarium hours:

Open 7 days a week from 9 A.M. to 6 P.M. See other side of brochure for contact details.

TICKET

Bluewater Bay Aquarium

ADMIT ONE

water Bay Aquarium

TIMETABLE

Don't miss the feeding frenzy!

	Where?	When?
🕘	Kelp forest	9:30 A.M.
🕚	Eel enclosure	11:00 A.M.
🕐	Penguin pool	1:30 P.M.
🕒	Shark tank	3:00 P.M.

Glossary

echolocation – a system of locating objects by listening to how long a sound takes to bounce back. Bats also use echolocation.

extinction – no longer living. If an animal is extinct it means that there are no more of that kind of animal alive.

food chain – a pathway of food supply. A food chain starts with a plant which is then eaten by an animal. That animal is then eaten by another animal and so on. Kelp forests are the start of the food chain for whales.

habitat – the natural home of an animal or a plant. A habitat can be as large as an ocean or as small as a pond.

herbivore – an animal that eats only plants

invertebrate – an animal without a backbone. Earthworms, snails, jellyfish, squid, octopuses and nautiluses are examples of invertebrates.

photosynthesis – the process in which a plant uses sunlight to change water and carbon dioxide into food

plankton – billions of tiny plants and animals that float in ocean water. They are eaten by larger animals as part of food chains.

species – a group of the same kind of animals. Animals of the same species have many features in common.

Index

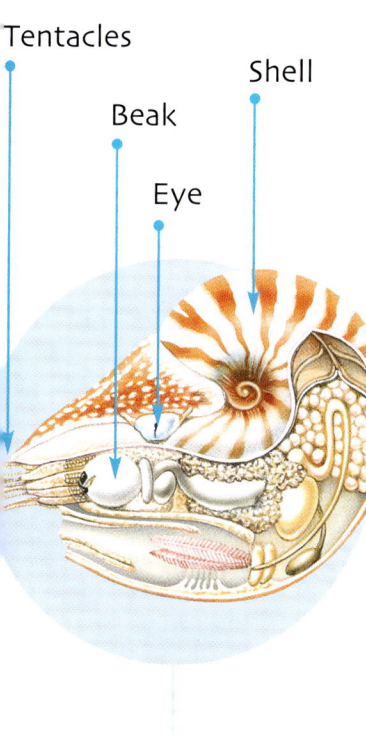

Tentacles
Beak
Shell
Eye
Nautilus

blubber	18
cuttlefish	10
dolphins	20, 22–23
drift nets	23
dugongs	26–27
echolocation	20
food chains	6–7
invertebrates	8, 21
jellyfish	8–9
kelp forests	6–7
photosynthesis	7
plankton	7, 15
mammals	14, 26
manatees	26–27
Melville, Herman	18
octopus, giant	10–13
sea otters	6–7
squid, giant	20–21
submarines	4–5
whales	6–7, 14–25

31

Discussion Starters

1 Take a look at the dolphins on the title page of this book. They are Indo-Pacific humpbacked dolphins that swim in the warm shallow waters of mangrove swamps and lagoons. How could you find out more about these dolphins?

2 In some parts of the world people harvest huge amounts of tiny sea creatures called krill. Krill and plankton are the main foods of great whales. What do you think might happen to the food chain if one part of it is broken?

3 People like to go whale watching. They even swim with mammals such as dolphins and manatees. Do you think these animals enjoy attention from humans, or do you think people should leave them alone? Why?